The YazooKeeper

TITLE: The Yazoo Keeper
By: Macklyn Austin
Edited by: 846 Global Publishing
Cover Design: 846 Global Publishing
Copyright 2023

The names of real people and other details have been changed to protect the identities of the people involved. This book is based on personal opinion, experience, and research. The following is based on my memory of events of my life story. I acknowledge that the memory of others may be different.

The author cannot be held responsible for the outcomes based on suggestions in this book. Always consult a professional before making any medical, legal, or business decisions. The author shall not be held liable or responsible for any loss or damage allegedly arising from any suggestion or information contained in this book. This work depicts actual events in the life of the author as truthfully as recollection permits.

Permission: For information on getting permission for reprints and excerpts, contact the author at:

macklyn@sbcglobal.net

The YazooKeeper

By Macklyn Austin

DEDICATION

I want to dedicate this book to my two loving daughters, who are the ones my life revolves around. My conscious decisions, thoughts, and plans are executed with them and their well-being in mind.

I hope and pray my life lessons and success carves out a path toward even greater success for them. They are literally my "Double A" batteries that keep my heart pumping. Being the man in their lives has helped me become a stronger wiser man.

Ava Grace and A'myracle, you will forever be the locomotives that power my existence and the inspiration that breathes life into me every day.

May God bless you both to be leaders and prosperous through life.

You will always be my greatest loves!

TABLE OF CONTENTS

Prologue

"I'd like to be a queen of people's hearts."

~ Princess Diana

At our publishing company, we call him The Mayor as in "Hey, when is our next appointment to interview the mayor?" Of course, we know he is not "the mayor." Not yet. He is Vice-Mayor or Mayor Pro Tem. But, as soon as I met Macklyn Austin, I felt like I was conversing with a great leader and an old friend. He could have been my brother, my cousin, or the mayor of my town. He was everything a person would want in a leader: calm, wise, strong, and winsome in the most magical way.

Then I heard his story and wondered how such an amazing spirit could arise from the depths of hell he had seen.

People often talk of the phoenix that ascends from the ashes and soars to great heights. But they rarely talk of how the phoenix uses those ashes. According to mythology, the phoenix is set ablaze, consumed by the fire, and reduced to ash. It does not spring up from out of the ashes. Instead, it uses the ashes to remake itself. The new phoenix is every bit a re-creation of the old.

That is what I see in Macklyn Austin.

Now that I know this chapter of his story, his life's struggles make perfect sense to me. But I didn't have to live through what he lived through. I didn't have to see what he saw and survive what he survived. But I, like you, am blessed to have been a beneficiary of his tenacity and overwhelming generosity.

The word "mayor" comes from a French word coined in the middle ages: *maire*. It simply means large. And when I say Macklyn is larger than life, I mean that he is larger than the life he has lived. Larger than the pain. Larger than the poverty. Larger than the hurts. Larger than the rejection. He towers over his past with the graciousness one would expect from a gentle giant on a mission to don his cape and save the world. And from his darkest places, he has been reborn to soar the heights.

Who knows but God what lies ahead for this incredible life? I can only imagine the best is yet to come. No matter what, he will remain a treasure in Yazoo City, a friend to everyone he meets, and the mayor of people's hearts.

Angee Costa
Biographer, CEO of 846 Publishing

Introduction – Life's Dream

"Hold fast to dreams,

For if dreams die

Life is a broken-winged bird,

That cannot fly."

— Langston Hughes

Nearly fourteen years separate me from the day I started this project to the day I finished it. Fourteen years. So much happened in that time period, I nearly lost my grip on the dream to tell my story. But there was a tug so deep in my soul to share what I have seen and heard, even the passage of more than a decade was not enough to extinguish the fire within.

A story about growing up in poverty is no great tale. Millions of people do. Escaping poverty is also rather common. We hear those success stories all the time. But the details of my past are so unusual, so bizarre, I can hardly believe it happened to me. As the old Black mamas used to say, "My soul looks back and wonders how I made it over."

Growing up, no one would have ever thought that I'd be where I am today. No one chose me as "most likely to succeed." I was not at the top of anyone's "who's who" list. Today, I am active in politics and looking toward a run to be the next mayor of my hometown in the next couple of years.

It was a period of six years that really catapulted me to the position where I am today. But it first took a decision on my part to accept that, in spite of my past, I was meant to be a leader in the community. Since that time, I have humbly served as the backbone of my town, finding places where my gifts could best be of use.

Whether you are religious or not, you may find that the words of Christ resonate with you when he said:

Let he who is greatest among you be servant of all.
~ Matthew 20:26

It is a principle I have lived by whether I am helping families financially, providing kids with school uniforms, or collecting and distributing clothes. My starter scholarship program gives away funds to less fortunate families of high school graduates. And every Thanksgiving I provide food plentiful enough to feed my entire city of 10,000 plus people. This is what a life of service is all about — seeking out needs and meeting them. It is something that has always been at the core of my heart and is what has propelled me into the positions I hold today in city government. And I love every minute of it.

I was shocked when doing what I love and what I do best caused people to see me as a leader and show their love for these simple acts of service. It filled me with so much joy that I could do what I enjoy and fulfill my destiny at the same time.

There was certainly no indication of my future in my difficult past. Some of the things that happened in my life were not just obstacles to overcome; they were actually ingredients in the stew that made me who I am. So often in life we look at our challenges as enemies because they are so arduous, painful, and traumatizing. I trust that what you read in the coming pages will challenge you to understand that your hardships are useful tools in your arsenal throughout your life. If you were abandoned, you know the value of commitment. If you were poor, you know the value of entrepreneurship and money management. And if you were abused, you know the value of love and tenderness.

My past has birthed in me a spirit of generosity that I spread over my little corner of the world. Yes, that helps me to help others. But I cannot deny the immense benefit I receive. I am able to meet amazing people who become lifelong friends. I get to serve a community I love. And I feel ten feet tall when I can make a difference in someone's life. But that only happened because I was willing to keep pressing forward.

If you don't give up, your dreams and your aspirations can come true. They have no expiration date. They may take longer to realize than you hope, but they never expire. That is the key many people miss. Perseverance is more important than any other quality. It trumps education, intelligence, personality, etc. Yes, you will need those things and more to succeed. But, if you quit before reaching the finish line, it won't matter how smart you are or how much you know.

Becoming the Yazoo Keeper has been a spiritual journey as much as it was emotional, psychological, familial, and social. The changes that happened deep inside where no one could see have made the most impact on my life today. I have had to learn to summon the deepest stores of strength through all those trials and tribulations that I went through. I finally came to a place where I had to stop looking around at my life and look up at my Source. I looked toward heaven and flatly asked God what my purpose was. Why was I even born? Was my life destined to be the miseries I had experienced or was there more to my life? I asked God for answers about my existence on earth and my purpose for being here.

It was a bold question to ask the Creator of the universe. But I needed direction. And I received just that! Suddenly, the path forward seemed to form ahead of me. It was a long, steep climb to pull myself out of the pits of the past. But, at the same time, there were lessons, wisdoms, and treasures from my past that I hope to never escape. Together, the good, bad, and the ugly formed the man I am today. Of course, I continue to ebb and flow. But I would not trade places with any other man in the world. I am strengthened by what I have endured and grateful that I managed to overcome.

For all my readers who, like me, grew up in poverty, some of what you are about to read will be familiar. After all, I started life as a poor boy in a small town. Even those who experience poverty in big city life will be able to relate. But even for those who had monetary wealth, there are a dozen different ways to be poor. Sure, there is poverty of finances. But that is nothing compared to poverty of intellect, poverty of opportunity, and poverty of spirit, will, drive, and determination. One can overcome financial poverty. But poverty of mindset can doom even the richest among us, just as wealth of mindset can take a man or woman from the valley to the mountaintop.

I still live in the hometown where I grew up. While others with a hard life seek to run from the place of their pain, I made a different choice. I decided to deepen my connection with my beloved Yazoo City and do all I could to help others have the best life they could. As an Alderman and Vice-Mayor of the town, it is my job. But as a member of this community, it is my honor.

Chapter 1 – How it all began

"There are only two ways to live your life. One is as though nothing is a miracle. The other is as though everything is a miracle."

— *Albert Einstein*

As a kid, I never liked going to school. For me, it was a bit of an oxymoron. There was this beautiful building filled with books and people with knowledge who were ready to impart their wisdom to me for free. At the same time, behind the big steel doors were bullies and pressures far too extensive for a little guy like I was back then to have to contend with. It never made sense to me that something so magical as education could exist alongside something as destructive as bullying.

I was only in third grade when I had my first severe experience with bullying. A kid decided he would pick on me each day as I walked back and forth to school. He was relentless, every day hunting me down so he could intimidate and frighten me. I was afraid to tell my siblings and mom. In my young mind, I somehow believed that my bully could harm them. So, I kept it a secret.

School was filled with endless temptations. In the very same place where you worked to set your life on a positive path, you could be offered some substance or opportunity that had the potential to derail you permanently. I could never reconcile those two inconsistencies. So, school became a turn-off. Thankfully, at least in the early days, I had home as a refuge.

I hailed from what I deemed to be a good family, though no one in my family was wealthy. There would be no rich uncles to die and leave me anything. And I would not be able to count on any kind of financial backing from family and friends. There would be no one to write the check for me to go to college. Everything I would get would have to be earned.

Somehow, though I can't explain it, I knew that I was supposed to be a leader and a pillar in my community. Even at a young age, there seemed to be a calling on my life. As a boy, it was just a soft whisper that remained in the back of my mind. But as I got older, the call grew louder and louder. I always heard that call and wanted so desperately to answer. Of course, back then, there was no indication that there was anything particularly special about me. And, even though I felt the urge to be a community leader, I had no idea how that could be done. People like me weren't leaders... at least, that is the lie I heard and almost believed.

The Yazoo City of my youth was a county town. It didn't have many of the luxuries of the cities that surrounded it. There was no urban city center or towering skyscrapers. There were just honorable people who took great pride in their work, whatever it was, and who loved their families. The entire city, in fact, was like one big family. Everyone knew absolutely everyone. We knew who was related to whom, who was dating whom, and how our lives were interconnected. Weddings and funerals were equally likely to bring out the whole town in celebration or mourning. Everybody cared about everybody else and took an interest in each other's lives.

Of course, as was the case with many cities in the 50s, 60s, and 70s, my hometown started taking a turn. And my family, sadly, was caught up in it. The town that had enjoyed harmony between the races for the most part started to split between blacks and whites.

Our town was and is the gateway to the Delta. So, people started choosing up sides in different regions and migrated apart from each other. There were acres of corn fields, cotton fields, soybean fields, and other crops. Many of the whites were heavily invested in the agricultural sector and moved onto farms in one part of town.

Still, the town was growing and started catching up with the rest of Mississippi. Major stores started coming to areas close enough for people to travel and shop. Schools were built or expanded. But there was a clear divide between the amount of investment on the Black side of town and the White side. We had only two high schools and two middle schools, but they were split along racial lines. The failing schools were the Black schools.

Thankfully, there were no overt acts of racial violence or major clashes between the races during my childhood. I don't even remember personally experiencing significant racism. But it was clear that the Whites had the upper hand because they were more financially stable in the early years of the town's settlement.

I was blessed to not have to be involved in the cultural changes happening in my community. I was just a boy and too young to understand what was happening at the time. My biggest concern was school and family. I wasn't influenced either way by it, because even though we knew there was a disparity, no one bothered anybody or offended anybody. The spirit of charity ran free in Yazoo City and was instilled in me at a young age.

Perhaps the greatest example of this was in my own home. I saw how my mother shared her limited resources with her neighbors and friends. I watched the things she did and gave to others. Many times, she would take money reserved for paying her bills to help someone in need. She was the first to teach me the spirit of charity.

In spite of the hardships of her life, my mother continued to be a beacon of light and love for me and for others. She understood that it was more important to give than receive. And she spent her entire life as a giver.

Chapter 2 – The Blessing of Motherhood

"Motherhood is a choice you make every day, to put
someone else's happiness and well-being ahead of your own, to
teach the hard lessons, to do the right thing even when you're not
sure what the right thing is...and to forgive yourself, over and over
again, for doing everything wrong."
— *Donna Ball,* At Home on Ladybug Farm

Perhaps the greatest advantage I have enjoyed is the love and guidance of a wonderful mother, named Shirley. I always felt safe with her. Her voice... her loving touch... her ever presence were the building blocks of my life. She offered the calmest expression of love.

Life for my mother wasn't easy. But as far back as I can remember, she worked hard to help the community while caring for me along with my siblings. I have four brothers and one sister.

Thankfully, she wasn't alone in raising us. For most of my childhood, we lived with my grandmother and uncle in the neighborhood of Jonestown.

A manual on parenting could have been written based on her life in those early years. I remember mom walking us to school from the time I was in head start all the way until I reached the fourth grade. And, dutifully, she was there every day after school. I couldn't wait until school was over and I stepped through those big doors to see my mom waiting for me.

As I think back on those times, I can't imagine how she handled it all. She worked numerous jobs in order for all of us to have everything we needed. Yet, she managed to be there for my siblings and me. Things seemed so perfect in my childhood. I felt I didn't have a worry in the world. In her care, I was always secure despite whatever was happening in life.

And there was plenty happening!

We had moved from my grandmother's home and to an apartment with my mom and all my siblings together. It was tight, but we were all close, so we made it work as best we could. Being the baby of the family, watching my brothers and sister fight a lot, I was able to stay out of the fray. My sister, being the only girl, was catered to a lot, but my mom still made sure we all were well-adjusted.

In actuality, we moved to three different houses throughout my childhood. Sadly, these were not always moves up! With each change in housing, it seemed that things were getting worse for my mom. For the longest time, I just didn't see or know what was burdening her. But I could see the effects of the weight and strain she bore.

She managed it all quite well, though, primarily because of her faith in God. She was a devoted Christian woman who took us to church weekly. We had the visual example of her faith and commitment to God. Church was fun. But the strength of her spiritual devotion was never lost on me due to the way my mother worshiped and served. She always made me cry whenever she sang at church. Her voice was like listening to an angel descended straight from heaven.

It wasn't until I reached the eleventh grade that her silent pain became our public shame.

My mother and father had gone their separate ways years earlier. And my mother was focused solely on raising her children. Later, though, she met a man and fell in love. As my mom's boyfriend, this man completely won me over. And he did the one thing my father refused to do: he asked to marry my mom.

My stepfather was a kind man, at least in the beginning. He seemed to understand the family he was coming into and wanted to take on the challenge. I was skeptical of him at first because I always wanted my dad to marry my mom. But my father never stepped up to his responsibility the way my stepfather did.

After the wedding, it was time for another move. My sister, two of my brothers, my Mom, and I moved in with her new husband. For the first year everything was perfect.

My stepfather was good to my mother and nice to me. I loved spending time with him, which I got to do often. In no time, he became like Superman to me. I grew to love the man because he did everything I wanted to do with my dad but couldn't. We spent many an afternoon fishing and hunting. He, along with my mother, took us to church, and we sat together as a family. He introduced me to sports and took me to football games. And we camped together, enjoying each other's company as we sat beneath the stars. My stepfather was there for all the important rites of passage in a young man's life, like being the one who taught me how to drive.

But soon after the first year ended, things turned for the worse. It started small and grew into something devastating and destructive to our family. For starters, my stepdad would discipline my sister and brothers in ways that were not pleasing or acceptable to anyone in our family. He found her to be rebellious and disobedient, deciding it was his place to set her straight. The result was that she rebelled more, and my stepfather alienated himself from the other members of the family. Even though I wasn't there to see it most of the time and my relationship with him was always positive, things had gotten bad enough that my siblings refused to live with him any longer. They packed and left to live with other relatives.

I was in a state of confusion. My stepdad never harmed me nor disciplined me the way he did them. He barely ever even scolded me for my behavior. I believe he was so fond of me because he had a son that was my age who died. I reminded him of that son he once had, and he saw an opportunity to reclaim those lost years by bonding with me. I was lucky. My siblings were not.

A few years of the marriage passed by, and I started to see changes in my mom. The light in her eyes faded. The spring in her step had dulled. It was obvious that her happiness was gone. She started to disconnect. Where she was once intensely involved in our schooling, she grew more passive and didn't push me hard like she had. Her main focus was saving her marriage by trying to please my stepdad. Together, they tried their best to paint a picture to the world that we were a perfect family.

We were far from perfect.

As time went on, I would occasionally hear the arguments. They were just whispers at first. But, over time, they grew louder and more bitter.

The arguing worried me. But, at the same time though, my mother and stepfather showed me love and did whatever they could to make sure I was happy at all costs.

But how could I be happy when the one I loved the most, my mother was not at all happy? None of that happiness meant more than my mom's happiness. I remember several times asking my mom if she and I could just pack up, leave, and not tell anyone. She smiled and continued to endure the hard times. No matter what, my mom wanted her marriage to work, because so many thought she shouldn't have gotten married anyway. She was constantly fending off the opinions of others who tried to put their input into her marriage. This forced her into an internal isolation where she felt she had to keep her feelings and experiences to herself.

Things between my mother and stepfather continued to worsen until that fateful day when I witnessed my stepdad curse my mom and threaten her. My first reaction was heartbreak for my mother and shock that my stepdad could speak to her that way. My second reaction was protective. I quickly ran to my mom's defense, standing between him and her. My stepdad was shocked and hurt that I had heard him disrespect my mom.

After that, my relationship with him was never the same.

In the midst of the turmoil occurring inside my home, another storm was brewing outside of it. My girlfriend announced that she was pregnant. I was just fifteen, but I was going to be a father. It was a tumultuous time when I really needed my mother's guidance. At first, the news of the baby brought a fresh sense of joy to the house. The coming baby brought a sense of calmness and happiness for my mother. By me being so young — just in the 11th grade — my mom poured the immense amounts of love and attention she had once had for me into my daughter. And seeing my mom happy again was one of the best feelings I had in years.

In the midst of the happiness from the new baby, the marriage problems seemed to build more and more and broke that steady air of joy. My mom's odd patterns were starting to get to the best of me. I couldn't focus on school because I was worried about her, worried about my girlfriend, and worried about how I could be a father. But it was my mother's happiness and well-being that weighed heaviest on my mind. I could see that she wasn't sleeping in her bedroom. And her thinning frame confirmed that she was barely eating.

Problems at home were rapidly escalating. Lights and water were being turned off intermittently for lack of payment. We stopped celebrating special events altogether. We didn't even have a normal Christmas for four years.

It was during my senior year that an even more devastating fight occurred that shaped our lives in the most tragic way. I was celebrating the fact that I had finally graduated from high school after some tough academic years. My mom was happy as she could be about graduation, and I wanted her to be there more than anything so that she could see that her work was not in vain. I was thrilled to see her out there cheering for me, not knowing that soon she would be removed temporarily from my life.

Over the years preceding this time, her marriage and family life had reached a breaking point. My mom had all she could take of my stepfather's cruelty. Their last argument and what followed caused me to lose my mother for many years.

An argument between them turned physical. He attacked her and my mother, otherwise defenseless, fought back against his assault by grabbing a pot of grease with one hand and boiling water with the other and throwing it on him.

I was not there. But the scene I found when I returned was horrifying. It was a true crime scene that told the story of pain boiled over into violence. That awful scene continues to give me nightmares when I am able to sleep, making me thankful for the sleepless nights that came for years. Seeing the furniture destroyed, blood stains everywhere, strips of human skin on the floor, and devastation from what looked like a horror movie, I knew my mom was hurt and in trouble. I could feel it and sense it.

My mother was arrested and convicted of assaulting my stepfather. She was sentenced to serve a long prison stint just for fighting back and defending herself from her husband.

My mother ended up going to prison for eight years out of her ten-year sentence. It was eight years of my life that I had to mostly live without her that started just after I graduated high school.

Being separated from her was one of the hardest seasons of my life to endure. But I did not know how difficult it would be to have to go to the prison to visit her. She was the calmest, most loving, and sweetest lady on earth. It nearly killed me to watch her fight to survive prison life. But she did so with great strength and dignity.

I made sure that whenever I couldn't visit my mom, I took the time to sit down and write to her. I sent her words of encouragement in those letters. And she would write back, motivating me to be all I can be in life.

The college years were especially tough. For starters, I was far away from home, away from everyone I knew and loved. There was no security blanket. I had to make it for the most part on my own. My mother wasn't there because she was still serving her prison sentence. And my father wasn't there because he chose not to be. I had to do this alone.

While I was in college, I saw a lot of things that were culturally shocking to me — things I had never seen before. They may not seem major to others. But to me, they were jarring. For example, when my classmates and I went to lunch, we would all sit down with our plates. I would devour every bite, thankful to have food. But they would throw food away. I couldn't believe my eyes. There were days when I was hungry still, but I didn't have money to buy more food. I would leave class early and go to trash cans, searching for food that looked clean enough to take out of the trash and eat.

No one knew how I was suffering because I always put on a happy face. I never told them I was eating from the garbage can, not wanting to be a burden on anybody. I am sure that, if they knew, they would have collected some money to send me. They would have moved heaven and earth to help me. But I was too proud and too ashamed to receive the help.

The person whose help I needed and wanted was my mom's. But she was locked away. And my world was incomplete.

After years in prison, my mom finally got released. She immediately started the process of putting her life back together. She remarried and got even closer to God and is now loving life once again.

Chapter 3 - Love is in the air

"I'm selfish, impatient and a little insecure. I make mistakes, I am out of control and at times hard to handle. But if you can't handle me at my worst, then you don't deserve me at my best."

— *Marilyn Monroe*

I was first introduced to sex at the tender age of five when my uncle carelessly brought a woman to our childhood home while the family was there and had sex with her. As a curious boy, I peeked through the keyhole of the old wooden door which was plenty wide enough to see everything that was happening. But I did not understand what they were doing. The impact of what I saw was burned in my brain and I couldn't shake the images. But the effects were obvious as I grew older and started to struggle with sex addiction as a kid.

I was a young boy living in a big house, so one of my favorite activities was to explore. I loved moving around that old house and seeing what everyone was up to. But I got more than I bargained for that day.

21

It just so happened that I was in the hallway and saw that one of the main big bedrooms was locked. Back in those days, the keys were gigantic as were the keyholes they fit into. So, it was easy for me to peek in.

Had I been an only child, I might have spiraled out of control immediately. But I was blessed with a large and loving family. So, even though the damage of my uncle's carelessness was done, it would be years before the real trauma surfaced.

With four siblings, of course, we had the normal, sibling fights and clashes. But there was nothing out of the ordinary. At least not in the beginning. But, over time, our ordinary turned quite extraordinary

My first real girlfriend was Myra. We were high school sweethearts. She wore these thick black glasses that just made her face stand out from the rest of the girls, and she looked so beautiful to me. Back then I was certain that I would be spending the rest of my life with her. But it was just puppy love between two school kids.

We found ourselves alone and locked in a passionate embrace. We were both virgins with no idea what we were doing. But she was looking to me for guidance since I had lied to her and said I was already experienced with sex. I said it partially from embarrassment but also to make her feel more comfortable and not scared to have sex with me.

Our times together grew more and more frequent and, just like my uncle, I got careless. I became bold and stupidly courageous as I sneaked in and out of her house while her parents were there. I didn't care. I just wanted to be in her presence and to hear her sing to me. I wanted to be close to her and was willing to risk whatever I had to. Once, at her house, her sister came home while I was there. I ran into the closet to hide. But she knew I was there and flung the closet door open, ordering me out of the house.

My relationship with Myra lasted well into my junior year of high school until my head was turned by another beauty. I hooked up with this new young woman, leaving Myra heartbroken by the unceremonious way I left her. I knew what I did was wrong. She didn't deserve it, and I paid the price for my mistreatment of her. I felt that what I did to her cursed me for every relationship I was in after her. Nothing seemed to work for me romantically, and I was sure that it was the residual effect of the pain I caused her. She moved on with her life and had a few kids. She's doing fairly well in life, and I couldn't be more happy for her.

Then there was Paula.

Paula and I were in the same grade together from head start through graduation. She could have easily competed with other beauties in our school as one of the prettiest girls in our city. Practically every guy in town had a crush on her and wished he could date her. I was among her admirers, but I never had the nerve to show interest in her because I felt I wasn't cool enough. I was sure that any attempt to date her would be met with laughter.

I finally built the nerve to ask her out, and it worked. She was interested in me as well. We spent the entire summer together, just walking around town hand-in-hand or sitting side-by-side on her parents' porch. She was most definitely a down-to-earth person and easy to talk to. The minutes effortlessly slipped into hours, and I could spend the entire day with her without realizing how much time had passed.

After our first summer together was over and school started back, she ended up going to a different high school than I did. I was so angry that my mom didn't let me attend the same school, I felt as if my life was over. I instinctively knew that attending separate schools would be the end of our relationship. I would lose her to some other guy she could see every day. And that is precisely what happened.

Eight years after high school, our paths crossed again. We were as enamored of each other as we were at the start and resumed a romantic relationship. This time I just knew we were destined to be together. After all, we had found our way back to each other. It must be destiny, I thought.

In the beginning, we were the perfect match. I had never been so deeply in love in my life. I just knew this would be the love that would last forever. At the time I had a fairly decent job and used every penny to do any- and everything I needed to do to keep a smile on her face. There were times when I would spend my last dollar or sacrifice my bill money just to impress her, pretending that I had it "going on" financially. Then the recession hit and the economy caused people in my industry to suffer. I lost my job and started to work odd jobs just to make a living and keep up with the lifestyle she had grown accustomed to.

When honorable and honest work was not enough to provide the things I wanted to give her, I turned to illegal means. I got caught up in drug dealing, illegal gambling, and many other things that could have landed me behind bars.

As time passed, I could see a change in her behavior. It started with the way she talked to me. Gone was the love, admiration, and respect we shared. It was replaced by anger and accusations of things that I didn't do — things I would never do. The most heartbreaking part of it all was when I found out that, since day one, she wasn't fully faithful to me. I felt like my life was over.

I started investigating to see what she was up to and discovered her many indiscretions. Things got so bad that I even caught her cheating numerous times. But my love for her overrode my shock, and I took her back. Worse, I even proposed to her because she made it seem that getting engaged would show my true love for her. I will admit that marriage was also my way of ensuring she would be with me.

One night after I left her house, I had a strange feeling that something was wrong. I circled back that same night and stood outside her window just in time to hear her on the phone with another guy talking about how much she loved and wanted him.

Devastated, I decided the only solution was to take my own life. I felt abandoned, betrayed, and worthless. This started a vicious cycle of suicidal thoughts that plagued me for years. Finally, I realized that I had to make a massive change if I was going to be able to let her completely go. I left my beloved Mississippi and moved to Houston, TX to live with my brother, Cortez. It was the only way for me to get peace of mind.

When I returned to Mississippi, I got back in the flow of life and work. It was time to make some money! But, in the midst of pulling my life together, my eye caught sight of a pretty light-skinned girl who sat at the front of the bus. Who would've known how my relationship with this girl would change my life. I would see her every now and then on the bus the rare times I rode it. But each time, I looked for her. Little did I expect that she would end up being the mother to my child.

When I saw her on the bus, she looked sad and a bit angry. She always sat in the front row of the bus, away from the noisy people in the back. Whenever I saw her, I would picture what it might be like to talk to her. I started working on my courage, hoping that I would one day be bold enough to speak to her.

I'm glad I waited to make my approach because I later learned the reason she always sat at the front: her mom was the bus driver. It would have been a major no-no to walk up to her and make my approach in front of her mom.

I would see her in different places around school. We were in the same schools through high school where I would see her at different ball games and just admire her from a distance. Even though I occasionally saw a smile on her face here and there, those moments of cheer were always short-lived. She generally wore a mean expression on her face that communicated to me and everyone that she was not to be messed with.

After years and other life experiences, I grew in my confidence with women. I finally built up the nerve to say something to her. I was as nervous as I could be. But approaching women was getting easier and easier. Besides, I asked myself what was the worst that could happen; she could say no. But the *best* that could happen would be if she said yes. And that is what happened.

I sent her a message, and to my surprise, she messaged me back. I didn't respond to her reply right away because I wasn't expecting her reply to my first message. I hadn't checked to see that she had answered.

As the first few days passed, we shared messages back and forth. I was always on the road working but talking to her or messaging her was the highlight of those long weary days. She energized me as we built a strong chemistry. But this relationship was different from all the others that had come before. It felt like a breath of fresh air.

I was a better person at that time and more ready for a relationship than I had been in the past. At this time, I had built myself up financially. I was healthier, wealthier, and wiser after the trauma of my past relationships and heart breaks.

Once I got home from being out on the road working, it was time for our first date. I was excited to see her and get to know in person the woman I had been communicating with over the phone. It was as good a date as any. I took her to a bookstore and bought her a bible. I think this was what sealed the deal for us. She knew I was someone who respected faith in God.

We were both head over heels in love. Nothing could keep us apart. Things were moving so fast that I asked her to move in together within a year. This was a first for both of us. Living with someone was new and exciting. But it was also challenging.

Like most relationships, there were good days and bad ones. But we had a secret weapon going for us: since I was working on the road, there was never enough time for the bad times to get really bad. When we were separated, we missed each other and couldn't wait to be together again. By the time we were sick of each other, it was time for me to go back on the road for work. So, it all evened out.

As we progressed, our relationship revealed and uncovered more and more. I learned so many things about myself that I had never known. Our relationship brought out anger issues I never thought I had. And the same was true for her as well. So many times, we would be at odds and ready to kill one another. Thankfully, God would step in and ease our storms.

27

The most tragic part of our relationship was when a devastating argument ensued between us, and things got physical. This was maybe the angriest either of us had ever been in our lives. We had reached a point of no return, and we both felt that the relationship was over after that.

As we were making our plans to part, we learned that we were expecting. At that moment, any and all of our bad feelings and immaturity quickly disappeared. We were both excited about the news and ready to step up as parents.

Things went back to normal after that with the occasional ups and downs. I got a promotion on my job and felt it was time for me to purchase my first home. We were both excited about this. I truly just wanted her to be happy and wanted to do everything I could for her. She was eager to make our house a home.

A year or so of relative peace went by before our old ways started to creep back in. It was then that we decided we would call it quits for good.

She gave birth to an angel of a daughter. I knew then that all the grinding and hard work I had put in over the years needed to double. I was determined to not allow my daughter to go through any financial hardships. She would have everything she needed and many of the things she wanted. Both of us were grateful and happy for the new addition to our family. But the loving connection this woman and I once shared was irreparably broken. We had grown apart and realized that we were better off just being friends and loving parents to our child. But, as we parted ways, I made a vow to her that I'll always love her and she'll never have to worry about anything in her life whether we're together or not.

The YazooKeeper

Chapter 4 - Missing Dad

"I cannot think of any need in childhood as strong as
the need for a father's protection."
– Sigmund Freud

My dad wasn't always around when I was a toddler. But whenever he came around, I thought he was the ultimate superhero. I never wanted him to leave and secretly prayed he would marry my mother and move into the house with me.

We were connected in many ways and disconnected in others. When I was born, my mother thought about what she would name me. She decided my first name should be my father's last name so that I would always have a connection to him. It filled me with joy to know that I had his name with me always.

Dad was handsome and cool. He loved motorcycles and had built quite a strong reputation as a hobby racer. He was known throughout the racing world as one of the greats and that made me even more proud to be his son. Besides that, he was a top-notch electrician in great demand for his services.

While I loved my mom with all my heart, I begged her for years to let me live with my dad. I thought that he had a lot he could teach me about being a man. I had so many questions. But, even more than that, I just wanted to be with him — father and son. It was clear they would never get back together, so I wanted to at least experience what it was like to have my dad in the house.

Finally, after years of wearing her down, when I reached the sixth grade, she let me move to Minnesota with him. Minnesota was another one of those magical places I had heard about, but never saw. Dad would always tell me stories about how pretty the snow was there and how it fell from the sky in sheets. He explained that people put away their cars and rode around in snowmobiles. It sounded amazing. Mississippi's hot weather would never allow for the kinds of activities a kid like me could do in Minnesota. So, I wanted to go.

Being so young, I idealized what living with my dad would be like. I have images of father and son having fun, fishing, hiking, tossing the ball, and having snowball fights. I envisioned us side-by-side on snowmobiles traversing the fluffy terrain. My eyes were soon opened to the reality of who my father truly was.

Living with my dad started off fine. We had a lot of good days at the start. But he wasn't accustomed to having a child to care for and the constant responsibility that meant for him.

When we got to Minnesota, we moved in with his girlfriend and her son. That quickly turned out to be a terrible experience. I was miserable living with them, and it was clear that I was not truly welcome. But I stayed silent. I didn't dare tell my dad nor let it show that I was unhappy because, no matter what, I wanted to be in his presence.

Then our housing arrangements started to unravel. Just like it was with Mom back home, Dad had his share of relationship problems. When he and the girlfriend were at odds, Dad and I were out. That led us to moving two or three times all around Minnesota.

When I called back home to speak to the family, I never told anyone back home about my living situation because I was scared I wouldn't be able to stay with dad anymore. Mom would have certainly insisted that my father bring me back rather than allow me to stay in the dysfunction of my father's life.

Finally, on the last move in Minnesota, we ended up living with a cousin of mine who I felt was more of a big brother to me. He was into pretty much everything I was into. But his addictions to drugs and addictions to women traumatized me in ways that stayed with me for years. I was caught in a vortex. I loved my cousin and finally felt I had someone to befriend me, and I was close to my Dad. But everything else about my life was trauma. And my cousin's habits were growing more and more dangerous.

I remember going into certain stores with my cousin. He would ask what I wanted. I would point to things I wished I could have and daydream about someday having them. But, when we got outside, he would hand me the things I pointed to after shoplifting it from the store. His stealing was out of control, and I was complicit. I knew what he was doing was wrong, but I was just so happy to have all the games and toys a kid could ever ask for. My parents couldn't afford to buy me the things my cousin was able to steal for me. So, I said nothing and returned nothing to the store.

My cousin's worst habit, however, was his constant drug use. He made drugs look so cool. I prayed the day would come when I was old enough to live like him.

My one saving grace was that the school system I was in was amazing. I was the only black kid in the entire school system. But Minnesota was much like Mississippi where people didn't focus on your race. The kids treated me well even though it was different for them to be around this black kid.

My cousin had this one lady friend who came to visit him often. She was sweet and loving. She treated me like my mom had, so I instantly fell in love with her. She was a lot like the mother I had left behind back home, and her care for me helped ease the ache of missing my mom. All the generosity and care and compassion my mom showed, this wonderful lady showed me.

Both my dad and cousin saw how attached I had become to her. I always wanted to be at her home and stayed over so often, I became just like one of her children, basically living with her and her daughter. Unlike what I experienced with my dad's girlfriend, this lady's family took me in as one of their own.

But, from time to time, I had to return to the bittersweet life I had living with my father and cousin. My cousin's drug addiction and woman addiction had gotten so far out of hand, it started affecting my dad's quality of life. He didn't want to be around it and started to complain about my cousin's influence on me. The partying my cousin was doing brought lots of strangers and loud music into the house which caused me to stay up late at night. By the time I got to school the next morning, I was exhausted and slept through all my classes. Being tired made me irritable. Things that I would normally overlook caused me to act out. One day a white girl pulled my hair, and I slapped her in retaliation. The moment it happened, I just knew something bad was going to happen to me. Even though I had not experienced the worst side of racism, growing up in Mississippi taught me that society valued Whites over Blacks and certainly sided with girls over boys. I imagined that I might be dead by the end of the day for breaking the unwritten rule that a black person couldn't ever harm or offend a white person.

I rushed home and told my dad that I was ready to go back to Mississippi and needed to go immediately. I called my mom crying and she insisted Dad put me on a train and send me home. I never told either of them why I needed to make such an immediate escape. My dad assumed I didn't like the cold weather and wanted to get back to the muggy warmth of Mississippi. I never bothered to correct him.

Years passed, and I would see my dad here and there. But the older I got, the less he came around. I also realized that my dad really never did anything for me in the ways a dad was supposed to.

As I grew older and continued to long for him, my father ended up hurting me more than he ever helped me. He used me, lied to me, and made my life more difficult.

One of the worst things that happened occurred after I bought a brand-new car. I loved it so much and had worked hard to be able to earn it. My father took my keys one day without my knowledge or permission, and went joyriding. He had a crash and wrecked my new car shortly after I got it. I was furious with him but expected he would do the right thing and pay me back for the damage he had done. But he didn't. His pride would not even permit him to apologize for what he had done.

When I became a man and my life was on track, I realized that I had never really heard loving words from my father. Dad was too ashamed to say how much he loved me and that he was proud of me. Deep in his heart, he knew that I became a better man than he was, but he couldn't bring himself to speak that aloud.

Despite his flaws, I love him. Nothing could ever cause me not to love him. He gave as much as he could give. I believe that he would give his life for me if he had to. So, I have committed to loving and caring for him until his dying day.

We always want the people we love to be the perfect version of the roles they walk in. But just like we each have a story, our family members have a story too. They were shaped by the lives they lived. The greatest gift we can give is love and acceptance.

Chapter 5 - Grandma Alice

"A grandmother is a remarkable woman. She's a wonderful combination of warmth and kindness, laughter and love."

~Unknown

Wow. Grandma Alice.

She served as the backbone of the family and beginning of us all. Everything I am today is due in large part to her. All of the family has impacted my life in a positive way, but we all learned everything we knew from her. Growing up, my Grandma was always hard on me. I misunderstood her intentions — even thinking that she hated me at times. I didn't understand her ways. For example, it seemed that she would sometimes purposely embarrass me in public. She could be tough and harsh.

But as I got older, the truth of her motive grew clearer and the power of her love blazed brightly. I could see that what she did was all for my own good. She knew more about the world than any of us and understood how strong we needed to be if we were going to be good and decent people. She was showing and teaching the power

37

and purpose of tough love so that we would survive. She knew that the world would not be easy on us and wanted her children and grandchildren to be prepared.

I had the pleasure of going to my grandmother's house periodically. She lived near the park, so there was always plenty of fun to be had playing there with my siblings and other kids from the area. She even let us stay out late. She always said we could play until the streetlights came on. When they popped on, we knew it was time to high tail it back to grandmother's house or face real trouble.

It was always fun whenever family came from out of town and there would be at least twenty of us in her two-bedroom house. And back then, family really meant something.

Words can't express the love I have for Grandma Alice and the deep levels of appreciation I have for all that she was in my life and the lives of my siblings and cousins. There is no substitute for a strong and loving grandmother. She is irreplaceable.

Despite my complaints about her strictness, she and I grew to be very close, and some of the other family members were jealous of the bond shared and the relationship we enjoyed. She defined tough love because she knew that she was sending her grandchildren out into a tough world. We all wanted to make her proud.

She was not one to mince her words and never had a problem correcting whoever needed correction and telling off whoever needed telling off. I know that I get my dedication and strength from her. What she poured into me are the treasure troves of strength and love that I draw from to this day. Where would be have been as a family without her?

She continues, even in her late 70s, to be a source of continual love and inspiration. Her commitment to health has afforded her those 70 years. She can out-exercise the entire family and is the eternal glue that holds the Austin family together.

Chapter 6 – A Miracle is Born

"Anyone who tells you fatherhood is the greatest thing that can happen to you, they are understanding it for what it truly is."

— Mike Myers

Of all the women I dated, Carla was the one who really captured my heart. Of course, it was just that childish love that fades with maturity and time. But, at the time, it was all I knew about love, and I thought it was everything!

She was the life of the party and immediately attracted my attention. She knew how to make it known that she was in the building. She was the most fun and outgoing person. Besides, she was hilarious and could always make me laugh. That made her a joy to be around. She was a bit outspoken for sure, but she always knew how to say it in a funny way.

Carla was in one grade higher than me but we ended up in a science class together. I never even spoke to anyone in the class because I just hated science. I should have known she liked me because every day she would pick on me. She made fun of me because I was always concerned about staying fresh and clean. I worked hard to have new shoes and new clothes.

One day, she asked a friend of mine to give me a note basically saying she liked me. That was the way it was done back then. Many relationships started with the passing of a love note. At first, I showed no interest because she had teased me so relentlessly. But I finally came to my senses because she was such a pretty girl. And it didn't hurt that she was the cheerleading captain.

I was going steady with Myra at the time, but we were on bad terms. Both of us were thinking about splitting. So, I kept one eye turned toward Carla.

She continued to pick on me, until one day she made a joke about Myra having to ride a bus while she drove a big, expensive SUV to school. This caught my attention. In my little brain, I felt like breaking up with Myra to go steady with Carla was like getting an upgrade. Myra had tired of me anyway. So, we broke up, and I called on Carla.

For a while, we were secretly together with only a handful of people knowing about our relationship. It was fun to date in obscurity and something I wasn't used to. She was a year older than me and was able to pick me up for school and drop me off every day. None of the guys I hung around with were getting this type of door-to-door service from the girls they dated.

Our relationship continued to grow and eventually became sexual. Shortly after Carla graduated, she told me she was pregnant with our child. It didn't really hit me at the time that the baby could be mine. We were just kids having fun. But the fun was over, and life was about to get real for both of us. The baby ended up being my daughter.

Becoming a father for the first time was, without a doubt, the most defining moment of my life. It helped to make me the man I am today. I needed to step up to the plate and become a real man.

When A'myracle was born, the world seemed to take a new shape. She was instantly my sunshine... my joy. By the time she was born, I was just 16 years old and in the 11th grade. My days of being young and running wild had to come to an end.

I looked at my life with new eyes. I had been hanging with the wrong crowd and being easily influenced by the wrong people. Those same people were the ones who tried to tell me to deny that the baby was mine. Carla had been dating some super light skinned guy. When the baby was born, she had a very light complexion and emerald green eyes.

But when I saw her, I knew the truth. I looked into those eyes and she gave me this stare that caused my life to flash before my eyes. I was instantly transformed. I knew that I had my first significant purpose in life, and that was to make sure she was always taken care of.

I worked hard to provide for her and will continue to do so. But it meant that I was not always there when I wanted to be. I was always so hard on myself for all the missed birthdays and holidays I had to sacrifice by being away on the road from her. But she never wanted for anything. I always made sure that anything she could possibly need or want, I could buy it for her.

When I struggled with mental health concerns and entertained suicidal thoughts and plans for myself, it was always the thought of her that brought me back from the brink. It was her smile, her laugh, and her future that always gave me the boost I needed to go on and the dedication it took to stay alive and never give up.

As a dad, it's hard seeing her blossom into a young lady now. She will always be my little girl even though she is growing by the day. I want to protect her from everything evil in the world. I know what the world and ungodly men would try to do to a beautiful young lady like her. I can only hope and pray that the life lessons I have taught her will mold her into the best woman she can be.

Carla and I have always had a strong friendship, though, at times, it was on and off. But we never let it affect A'myracle. She now has three other children who I regard as my own. I love them all today and forever.

Chapter 7 - Brother Cortez

"Being his real brother I could feel I live in his
shadows, but I never have and I do not now. I live in his glow."
— *Michael Morpurgo, Private Peaceful*

Cortez is the oldest of all my mom's kids. Cortez and Quin had the same father and were born one right after the other. Cortez was another superhero in my life as a little boy. He was a great brother and loved spending time with me. He would always take me to different places with him. We had to walk everywhere we went. Sometimes, as a little guy, I would get tired. Cortez would lift me in the air, hoist me onto his shoulders, and carry me so I wouldn't have to walk.

His love for music and the school band made our household so loving and fun. There was always music and excitement over some upcoming event. All of the children in the family followed in Cortez's footsteps and joined the school band. The days dancing to the rhythm

45

of the drums and music will always be imprinted in my mind.

Band was like a breath of fresh air in our entire household. It brought immediate and abundant energy as my brothers, and later, I, practiced music and dances.

Cortez was always the source of life and laughter for us all at home. He did the best he could to be a true big brother. I knew that I would spend my life modeling him as I grew up. No one expected what would ultimately happen to my dear brother.

It started with marijuana. I hated to see my brother start smoking weed with his friends. He seemed to be above such activities and always seemed to want to set a good example. But the opposite happened when two of my other brothers followed in his steps as well by starting to do drugs.

Cortez and his friends would get so high, it changed their personalities completely. He wasn't the same fun-loving brother, full of energy, and always embracing his family with his charm and wit. He was tired and distant. He was often moody. My brother's drug addiction set him on a quest for the next high.

Cortez finally got old enough to leave the house. As much as I loved him, it was a relief to see him go. He went on to join the Job Corp. It did good things for him. When he came back home to visit, he always brought that same love, joy and laughter we loved about him.

After Job Corp., he moved to Houston Texas and lived with my Uncle Pat until he got on his feet. Even though he was relatively far away, he always called me to make sure I was okay. He would send me video games to whatever systems kids were playing on at the time. I was always grateful for the things he did.

Over the years, I went to visit him often. Then, when I moved to Houston for college, I was able to go over to Cortez's home even more frequently. It was always home away from home whenever I was with him during those college years. He made sure I was always comfortable and taken care of.

But it seems that Cortez, like everyone I was close to, had their share of trials and tribulations. Cortez's came in the form of intense legal battles with a company he worked for. Even though the court case seemed so promising, things didn't go in his favor. My brother was never the same after that. I felt like I lost the happy-go-lucky brother I had come to know.

But he quickly took advantage of his miserable state and got to work changing his life for the better. He became what some people called "woke,", increasing his sensitivity to and awareness of social justice and cultural issues. At the same time, he grew more in touch with his spirituality. This caused him to both lose and gain friends.

But he could never lose me. No matter what, I made sure our friendship and love remained intact no matter which direction in life he took. We still talk every other day, sharing inspirational advice with each other. He helps me to stay lifted and in high spirits.

Chapter 8 - Brother Quin

"Our brothers and sisters are there with us from the dawn of our personal stories to the inevitable dusk." —Susan Scarf Merrell

Quin was the second oldest of my mom's children. Unlike the rest of us, Quin was the quiet one. But that didn't mean he didn't have the bloodline accessible to him when he needed it. When the time is right and he wanted to, he could quickly become the life of the party.

Quin was probably the biggest sports fan of the family and was the first to introduce me to the game of basketball, which I grew to love so dearly. As a young boy I always imagined Quin going on to play college ball and, perhaps, going pro and playing in the NBA. I loved going to the park to watch him play ball and hear my friends say, " That's Mack's Brother." It made me so proud.

Whenever I was playing alone outside, Quin was always the one who would run outside, grab a bat, or pick up a ball to play with me. Once Cortez left home, Quin followed shortly after, moving to Chicago with his Dad.

Even though I was sad to see him leave our home, I could see that our stepfather and Quin had a rocky relationship. I could never understand why my mother's husband didn't like Quin. I would occasionally hear my stepdad say he hated that Quin had long hair like a woman. It was a cruel thing to say. Besides, I didn't see anything wrong with Quin's hair. He was the one who inspired me to grow my hair out for cornrows as a kid and my stepfather never said anything about my hair. He was just the kind of person who decided who he would love and who he wouldn't; those whom he didn't love caught his wrath or bitterness. It was enough to drive Quin out of our home.

Later, Quin moved to Houston where Cortez and I were living. I was sure that they were going to become like Batman and Robin. But their relationship seemed to be toxic, even though there was always love between them. Besides, Quin stayed so busy, no one really ever knew what was going on in his life. I always said that as long as I knew he was alive and well, I was willing to accept not seeing him more often.

Quin's difficulties in life centered around drug addiction. Once he got hooked, he was always engaged in the struggle to overcome the hold they had on his life.

My hopes and dreams for Quin is that he will become the man he always talked about being when we were growing up.

Chapter 9 – The Jurie is in

"Brother and sister, together as friends, ready to face
whatever life sends. Joy and laughter or tears and strife, holding
hands tightly as we dance through life."—Suzie Huitt

Jurie was the only girl of our crew, and like most "only" girls in any family, she pretty much got her way with things. We all favored her as a daughter or sister. It never bothered us growing up that she got away with everything because she had our love and support. But Jurie always had the upper hand, and everyone knew it and accepted it.

Even though she was older than me, I felt that I was her protector. I especially wanted to protect her from guys she dated. There were a few occasions where I got into physical altercations with a couple of guys she dated who didn't behave themselves. I wasn't afraid to stand up to them. All I cared about was her safety.

As we got older, though, I felt a sense of jealousy coming from my sister. It seemed to me that once my mom married, and my stepdad showed me extra love and attention, that my sister hated it. She hated <u>me</u> for it.

Worse, my stepfather was very tough on Jurie and wasn't tough on me. It threatened to drive a wedge between us.

Jurie was maybe the funniest and most playful of us in the early years of our childhood. She would always have something funny to say or something interesting to talk about. She and I had our own special bond. We would always watch comedy movies and shows together and then act out the funny parts in front of family.

Jurie was what you would also call a church girl. Like my mom, she had the voice of an angel when it came to singing and everyone loved to hear her. You could always hear the spirit and power in her voice whenever she sang.

As my only sister, I love her dearly. I loved her then. I love her now. And I will love her forever. Nothing will ever change that. Still, there was a major shift that weakened our bond when I had my daughter. I was so young and inexperienced — still in high school at the time. All of the family's attention turned to me. I noticed that she resented all of the care my daughter and I suddenly required of everyone.

A year after my daughter was born, Jurie had a daughter of her own. Today she also has a son and is enjoying her life in Texas. She is one of the most awesome mothers to her kids and to other peoples' kids that you could ever imagine. I couldn't be any more proud of her and thankful for the love she showed my daughter. I'll forever be grateful for that.

Jurie has now become the heartbeat of our family. Over the years she has borne the weight of all our family issues and burdens. When it comes to superheroes, she is a true modern-day Wonder Woman and forever will be just that in my eyes. She's definitely heaven-sent. I couldn't imagine what my life or my brothers' lives would be without her.

She is an amazing sister. But she walks in many roles as a mother and friend. I am so thankful that God chose our family to be the one she was born into. We have our memories to share for the rest of our lives.

Chapter 10 - Brother Drew

"From the time we're born, our brothers and sisters are our collaborators and co-conspirators, our role models and our cautionary tales."—Jeffrey Kluger

Drew was the third child in the bunch to be born. Well… technically. He and my sister, Jurie, were twins. Drew was always Mr. Suave and Debonair. He was the true ladies' man my friends and I wanted to be. He was always clean cut, well dressed, and almost always in a cheerful mood. If he was in a good mood, he was fun to be around. But he had the worst temper of us all.

He was the second to become a band freak in the family. His love for drums was second-to-none. Just like Cortez, he was devoted to the band and very talented. Whenever you saw Drew, he was always tapping and beating on something. He never wanted to be far from the beat.

My relationship and bond with Drew was just as tight as it was with my other brothers, but, for some reason, I felt like Drew was a better protector over me than the rest. He was always looking out for me and the rest of the family, doing his best to keep us all safe and out of trouble.

It turned out that he needed a protector of his own.

Things took a turn for the worst when Drew got introduced to drugs at a young age. So much so that he ended up getting diagnosed with schizophrenia. Being under the same roof as him, seeing him speak to ghosts or talking to himself was incredibly traumatizing to me. It reached the point that I was afraid to walk past him. I certainly never wanted to be alone at home or in the dark when he was there.

As years passed, his mental disorder made him more violent and disruptive. But whenever he was in a good mood, he's always a pleasure to be around. When he was going through an episode, he was terrifying.

Everyone loves him so much, especially Grandma. She, along with the rest of the family, continue to pray for Drew and hope things get better for him throughout his life.

Chapter 11 - The Cousins

"Cousin by blood, friends by choice."
Darlene Shaw

Cousin Richard

Cousin Richard was my Uncle Richard's son. When his family moved to Mississippi from Yazoo, we were as much friends as we were related. I had already had a few close childhood friends when I first met my cousin; but he was all of them wrapped up in one. We literally hung out almost every day. For sure, we spent every weekend together. Over the years of our childhood, we built an everlasting bond. He was there for all the fun times, but he was also there whenever I needed someone to have my back.

Once, a group of guys tried to jump me, and Richard ended up getting caught up in the crossfire. I felt so sorry and sad that he ended up in my mess. But we made a vow to each other that, no matter what, we would always take care of each other. He proved it by putting himself on the line to defend me.

The entire family believed that Richard was going to become a huge football star. His talent on the field was unmatched. Even though he didn't get to live his childhood dream of making it to the NFL, I was proud to see his face and name in the sports newspaper in our town. As we grew older, I was even more proud of the love and dedication he has shown for the youth of Yazoo City as he faithfully dedicates his time to teaching kids the game of football. The impact he is making in the lives of kids is priceless.

Lil Mike

Lil Mike was my Uncle Mike's only son. Even though my other cousins and I were like brothers, Lil Mike and I had a bond that was just a bit tighter than the rest. I was someone that he looked up to, and we couldn't wait until the holidays rolled around because that was a time we could expect to link up.

He and I shared a love for the game of basketball, which only made our relationship that much closer. A few years after I moved to Memphis to live with Mike and his dad, Mike's life took a turn that no one would have ever expected. Like most family members, everyone assumed Mike would one day be successful. Most of us thought he would become an engineer or some other type of professional.

Boy, were we wrong.

I had been dealing with my relationship problems with the young lady I was seeing. Mercifully, Mike took me on the road with him to California. I was so excited because I had always wanted to visit the west coast. When I jumped in the car, a beautiful woman was already there, and I learned she would be traveling with us. I didn't know what the reason for the trip was until we made our first stop in New Mexico at a hotel.

I assumed the woman was his girlfriend, so I didn't think much of the fact that she was there. But when we stopped and got our first hotel, Mike and I had our own room, and the girl had her own. At this point, I was confused. I questioned him and asked what was going on since I assumed he would be in the room with her. I'll never forget the words he told me:

"Cuz, this is what I do, and this is how I get my money."

The words hit me like a ton of bricks, and it all became clear. He was a pimp and the woman was a prostitute. It never would've crossed my mind in a million years that he would do such a thing. It felt like something you only see in movies.

I never told Mike that I was ashamed of him and sorry for the girl. But that was their lifestyle. They loved it and embraced it. I didn't agree with what he was doing. Still, I had made a commitment to protect him at all costs. He was my little cousin, and now he was in a world that I knew was dangerous and could cost him everything — including his life.

Along the way on our trip to California, we made dozens of stops. The amount of money that he and the young woman were making was mind-blowing. I had to find out more about her.

I waited until Mike wasn't around and asked the girl what made her choose this lifestyle. She was so gorgeous, I could imagine that she could have any man she wanted. She could have easily been a Hollywood actress or a New York fashion model.

She told me that when she was young, she would usually be home alone. One day, the UPS delivery person brought a package to the house. When she opened the door, he forced his way in and sexually assaulted her at a young age. The trauma of that incident somehow warped her mind and led to her choosing the escort lifestyle.

Her story was heartbreaking to hear. Here and there, I tried to encourage her. I assured her that she was beautiful and strong and that she didn't deserve what happened to her. I challenged her that she did not have to do the things she's doing for my cousin — selling her body and soul through sex for money. But she responded that it was all she knew.

When we made it to California, I was so happy to finally lay my eyes on such a magical place. But as I looked at it more closely, it wasn't what I thought it would be. Everything was expensive, and the people weren't warm and friendly like what I was used to in Mississippi or Tennessee. The whole place felt fake — nothing compared to what was shown in the movies.

We stayed there for a few weeks, but I couldn't bear to see this girl continuing to do the things she was doing. I had a daughter and all I could think about was what I would want someone to do for her if she found herself in such a horrible state.

I had to get away from it all.

I ended up catching a three-day long bus ride back home, but it was the best trip I ever had. Mike hated to see me go. But he needed to handle what he was doing. I wanted him to be safe and careful, but I couldn't condone the behavior or be present to watch any more of it. I pray to this day that God changes his ways for the better.

Cousin Walter

Cousin Walter, or Lil Walter as we called him, was the most unique person in the family. He was the most hilarious of all my cousins. You could hear him coming a mile away with his big voice and heavy country accent. Even though he was much younger than me, he behaved as if he was a big cousin to everyone. Everyone loved him and he was the life of every party or family gathering.

Sadly, I received the news of his passing and cause of death. This news really hurt the entire family. I can still hear his voice and often chuckle at his jokes. At times, it feels like he never left. No one in the family is really ready to accept that he's gone. It's a loss we will grieve for a lifetime. I felt life was unfair to extinguish such a bright life. But I just know I couldn't give up. I know that is not what Walter would have wanted.

Cousin Teon

My cousin Teon was maybe the closest thing I had to a younger brother. He looked up to me even though he never wanted to admit it. The first time I saw Teon was when his family moved in across the street from us in the home where my cousin Richard lived. We instantly clicked as family and friends. He was really a total reflection of me. Our friendship grew so close, I started to spend more time with him than I did with Richard. We did just about everything together — from playing ball, riding our bikes all over town, spending the night at each other's houses, and all the other fun things country boys liked to do. You would rarely if ever see one of us without the other.

After I moved away from Yazoo to go to college, we remained in close contact. But, as is the case with time and distance, our relationship wasn't the same. But we never lost our love and connection even when we didn't see each other often while living in different states.

On my college graduation day, my dad showed up to my graduation. But there was a young man standing beside him: Teon. I was overcome with joy and couldn't have been happier seeing him. It was the best graduation present I could receive.

Years after my graduation, Teon and I grew apart. I was starting to chase my dreams and better myself, but it seemed as if Teon really didn't have much interest in growing up. He was clinging to the old life we had. But I was coming into my manhood and just couldn't do the old things we once did as we were coming up.

These days, it's hard to get him to come over to watch a game or have dinner. I feel he is ashamed that he is still struggling and it's difficult for him to see me doing so well. I made it out of the ghetto, and he's still very much in it.

No matter what, though, our bond will remain the same. I would do anything in my power to help him.

Chapter 12 - Uncles are Superheroes

"We love our superheroes because they refuse to give up on us. We can analyze them out of existence, kill them, ban them, mock them, and still they return, patiently reminding us of who we are and what we wish we could be."
— *Grant Morrison, Supergods: What Masked Vigilantes, Miraculous Mutants, and a Sun God from Smallville Can Teach Us About Being Human*

Uncle Tyrone

Uncle Tyrone was the oldest son of my grandmother. Growing up, Uncle Tyrone was another one of those superheroes in my life. Whenever he came around, it was sure to be fun times. He was in the Air Force and would share with us the many interesting things he did and saw. I loved to hear all the stories and experiences he had to tell.

Uncle Tyrone put everyone at ease and was like a peacemaker. He would always do whatever it took to make any environment and situation a peaceful and happy one.

On those glorious days when he came home on leave, he couldn't wait to take the entire family out for shopping and literally let us choose anything we wanted.

Sometimes, I got to go and visit him on summer vacation or spring break. I longed to be one of his sons as I watched the things he did for his children and wife. He was a true family man and a loving father. The things he did for his family were things I could only dream about experiencing.

I so emulated him, I wanted to join the Air Force myself just so that I could follow in his footsteps. After I graduated high school and the incident with my mom happened, I was left without a parent to take care of me and was sent to go live with my uncle Tyrone. At that troubling time, I didn't know what direction my life was headed in. But my uncle was right there by my side, trying his best to get me into the Air Force.

Unfortunately, I was rejected by the Air Force due to 9/11 rules about being a single father. When I got word that I wasn't accepted, it broke me. I cried so hard in my uncle Tyrone arms, my entire body shook. All I wanted was to join the Air Force and start a family like he did.

But Uncle Tyrone was there to encourage me to keep dreaming and believing in an amazing future. Even though I couldn't join the Air Force, there were ways I could make an impact in the world. He helped me get my first job at an electronics store and taught me the importance of working. He advocated the theory of crawling before you walk in an attempt to teach me that it was okay to make small strides toward a big goal.

I can remember him saying it wasn't God's plan for me to be in the Air Force and that one day I would find my purpose. I really didn't want to hear that, but I still listened and took in all of his sage advice. It turned out that he was right. I had a different path to walk. To this day, it is those small talks with Uncle Tyrone that played a pivotal role in bringing me where I am today.

Uncle Charles

I was so fortunate to have so many superheroes. Another one of them was my Uncle Charles. Since my father was absent, Uncle Charles played the role of a father figure more than an uncle to me. Like Uncle Tyrone, Uncle Charles had many rich life experiences. I loved when he told stories and never tired of hearing them. Uncle Charles was in the military as well. But he went to the Army.

Uncle Charles was different from all my uncles. He played so many roles in the lives of so many people. He was the one who taught me the important lessons of what defined what a man was, how a man should treat and discipline his kids, and what it meant to love and (sometimes) spoil them at the same time.

I got to spend a lot of time in the summers with Uncle Charles and his wife. It was during those times that he instilled in me the important lessons of the power of wealth and hard work by showing me how the wealthy live. I was invited to go on drives with him where he would take me into million dollar neighborhoods. Uncle Charles knew the value of each property and talked about what people did to acquire them.

Those lessons he taught me helped made me understand the importance of perseverance and dedication. I learned that anything is possible. He also taught by example as I witnessed Uncle Charles enjoying some of the finer things in life.

Like everyone, he had his share of ups and downs. There were lean times when finances were challenging for him, but he never wavered in his commitment or faith. My uncle is a very spiritual man. His love for God helped me build my spiritual muscle and grow my faith in God. But it is his strength and fight that he continues to have that shows me that having faith God can and will turn your life around.

Uncle Mike

I believe that Uncle Mike was the fourth oldest of my grandmother's children. I would say Uncle Mike was the Superman of them all. I mean that both literally and figuratively. The strength in his muscles matched the strength in his heart.

Growing up with Uncle Mike meant good times were had by all as soon as he arrived at the family gatherings. Just like his brothers, he cared about everyone in the family and wanted us all to have a good time when he was around. I would say he was the most comical uncle of them all. But he wasn't all fun and games. His work ethic and determination were the biggest that I took from him. Watching my uncle work hard labor jobs in all kinds of weather to provide for his family was exactly the example I needed to see. I modeled his pattern of hard work and commitment. Every job I've ever had when I was younger was hard labor. Whenever times got tough on my job, I remembered how hard Uncle Mike worked.

With his inspiration pushing me, I continued to work no matter how difficult it got or how much it physically hurt.

He and my Aunt Mary have always been good to the family and the rest of my siblings when we were small. They came to get us any and every chance they could so that we could enjoy fun times with them.

The most impressive of all about Uncle Mike was watching him battle and beat cancer. He went through that tough time and then went right back to working hard. That's when I knew for sure he was the Superman of the family. He didn't need a cape to prove his superhero status. He earned it by the life he lived.

Uncle Curtis

Every family needs its historian and genius. For our family, Uncle Curtis was the Einstein of the family. The wisdom and knowledge that came out of his mouth every time he spoke would always leave me amazed. He was the perfect combination of knowledge and wisdom. He wasn't one for the trivialities in life. I never saw him watch much TV. He wasn't beholden to the sports culture. Instead, his head was always in a book.

In my younger years, he relentlessly preached to me about the value of a good education. In his mind, there was nothing that was more important.

One of the favorite things about Uncle Curtis was his generosity. Whenever he would come around, he would immediately reach into his pocket and give all the kids money without anyone even asking him to do it. I would often say to myself, "I guess that's what you can do when you have a good education."

As I got older, I found out firsthand that the words he spoke about schooling were right. Education became the key to any great job I got and it formed a stable foundation for me.

Uncle Curtis became a highly respected author, doctor, and historian. And it was after reading his book that I knew I was destined to be an author one day as well.

He was also the devoted father of one daughter. I watched him carefully, noting the way he cared for and interacted with his daughter to help me learn how to teach my daughter and raise her to be a young lady.

Uncle Pat

Uncle Pat was the youngest of them all. Just like me, he was the baby of the family. Uncle Pat was also highly athletic. He also helped me grow in my love of the game of basketball. Our relationship wasn't the typical uncle - nephew relationship. He was more like an older, wiser brother. He was hard on me, but I appreciated his style because he never made his scolding like a punishment. He wanted me to succeed in whatever it was I had a love for, and he talked to me about the things that mattered to me.

The summers I spent with him taught me to be tough and stand up for myself. He would never let me nor my other cousins play basketball with people our age; he always had us play ball against adults and more skilled older kids. He knew that beating kids our own age would not help us grow as players. I thought it was torture at the time because I had to work so hard on the court. He stood on the sidelines watching as these fully grown men knocked us around and pushed us over. But as time went by and I got older, I saw exactly what he was trying to teach us. He was using basketball as a metaphor for life. The lesson was that life isn't easy, and there is always someone out there bigger, better, and stronger. He wanted us to learn that when we got knocked down, we needed to immediately get back up, dust ourselves off, and get back out there, giving our all. This lesson remained etched in my mind for my entire lifetime. And I was able to confirm that it was true: when I gave my all, life got better for me.

Uncle Richard

Uncle Richard was my uncle on my Dad's side and was dad's older brother. I didn't get introduced to him until I was around ten years old because he lived in Minnesota. When moved from Minnesota to Yazoo City with his family, we got a chance to meet.

His son, Richard Jr., and I were the best of friends. If there was anything closer than brothers, that was what Lil Richard and I were.

Uncle Richard was a principled man and lived by one immutable law: hard work. It was the one lesson he drilled into our heads on a near-daily basis. Hard work. Hard work. Hard work. He believed that a man should work until he was tired. And then, when he was tired, that was the time to work the hardest.

To deepen our understanding, he always had chores for Lil Richard and I to do. For example, he would send us out to cut grass in the summer at the hottest time of the day. He never showed us any slack or mercy.

Lil Richard hated it most of the time, but it didn't bother me much. I had already had lessons about hard work from other members of the family, so I was accustomed to it. Even though I was young, I watched how my uncle raised his family and respected him for it. He proved that hard work could pay off.

That one lesson is worth its weight in goal because it allowed me to deal with life's financial struggles when they came my way. Whenever I didn't feel well enough to go to work, I was reminded of the times he would make his son and me push through sickness or pain. He believed that, if it didn't kill us, that we could get through anything. He had a huge impact on my life and others. I still apply that lesson of hard work today.

Chapter 13 - A Friend in Deed

True friendship multiplies the good in life and divides its evils. Strive to have friends, for life without friends is like life on a desert island... to find one real friend in a lifetime is good fortune; to keep him is a blessing.

Baltasar Gracian

KC

KC was my oldest brother's classmate and friend. My brother and he were very close. KC became a close friend of our family. Since he was friends with my brother, he was at our home a lot. As the years passed, KC and I developed our own friendship. He shared my love of community and charity, so we started doing community projects and service work for Yazoo together.

Whenever we were together, we talked about what we could do to be a blessing to the city. We had so many grand things planned and in store for Yazoo City.

71

Sadly, we would never get to live out those plans together.

I'll never forget the day I found his lifeless body at the bottom of a swimming pool. This was a month before my cousin Walter passed.

That experience changed my outlook on life. From that day to this, I never take anything for granted. I learned to show love every single day because tomorrow is not promised to any of us. KC's death taught me that none of us knows when our time may come.

Willie

I met Will in 2015 while I was in the midst of living a wild life and trying to not live it at the same time. Willie was many of the things I was still striving to become. He hailed from a churchgoing family just like me, but he continued his commitment to the church into adulthood. He was a man who could easily make friends within seconds.

Unfortunately, what brought us together was not as noble. Like me, we were caught up in all types of illegal gambling. We were only doing it just to get ahead financially and take care of our families. But we both knew the consequences of the things we were doing and wanted to get away from that life. We talked often about getting that one big break so we could hang up the illegal activity for good.

Thankfully, God had His hands on me and started to shift things in my life. I no longer wanted to be a part of that life. I started to see how it was bringing such negativity in my life. I received so much hate and envy from people I had the utmost respect for. I didn't want to go through life having to watch my back.

Willie and I finally set aside that part of our lives and encouraged each other as men. He is like a big brother to me. I can't count the number of times he's uplifted me. So much of our lives is parallel even down to our children.

It's a blessing to have a friend you can truly depend on no matter what. I absolutely know that if anything was to ever happen to me, he would step up and be there to make sure my family was ok. And, of course, he knows that I would do the same for him.
Friends like these were priceless in a young man's life. The bonds we forged as kids remain with us to this day.

Spencer

Spencer and I started out as classmates. We had always had a cordial friendship, but we didn't become like brothers until the 11th grade. Once we became close friends, we were inseparable even though we were so different. Spencer came from a well-off family. His father was even able to buy him a tricked-out sports car in the 11th grade. But you would never know that his family had money. Even though he was financially stable, he never was arrogant nor cocky in any way. He was just an all-around nice guy.

Spencer had started picking me up for school and dropping me off every day. It was so much fun to cruise around the city in that amazing car as we talked and laughed. It wasn't long before we drew the attention of many of the girls in town and thought of ourselves as "ladies' men." We didn't care who or how many girls we talked to and dated. We just loved going out with them.

I can't count the number of times Spencer came to my rescue when I managed to get myself caught up with a girl and her boyfriend. Spencer was always just one call away when some guy got jealous and wanted to pound me into the dirt.

Spencer was with me when my daughter was born, and I asked him to be her godfather. Our bond of friendship seemed unbreakable. We both have secrets that we will take to the grave.

Unfortunately, every friendship is not a friend to the end. Sometimes, sadly, the poor choices we make can cost us friendships that were meant to last a lifetime. To this very day, I carry the weight and pain of betrayal of one of my closest friends: Spencer. He was dating a girl who became his high school sweetheart. She had the key to his heart, and I believe that he loved her dearly. But my heart was drawn to this girl, and I harbored a secret love for her. It wasn't intentional. It just happened. The way I handled it, however, was not indicative of a good friend.

She saw me as a dear friend and would find comfort in me whenever she had problems. Those problems were usually related to Spencer. Every time they had a fight, she turned to me. Whenever he cheated on her, lied to her, or did her wrong, she ran to me. I was always there to tell her everything would be alright. In truth, I never guessed that, by her confiding in me, it would cause us to spark an interest in each other. There she was crying on my shoulder and our emotions got the better of us.

I went behind my best friend's back and secretly started dating his high school sweetheart: his first love.

Even though he wasn't innocent because of the way he treated her, I was worse by betraying a friendship.

I was so glad I had to move away after graduation so I wouldn't have to see or deal with her anymore. My heart broke for the ways in which I let Spencer down. I pray one day I will have the chance to talk to him and apologize for what I did so that I could be free from that weight I've carried for all these years.

We learn so much from our friends. They are the family we choose. But when we are blessed to have a friend whom we love and honor, we must also be willing to be loyal and show respect. It is so easy in this world of Facebook "friends" and fake connections to forget that true friendship is hard to come by. When we are blessed to have it, we must cherish it.

Chapter 14 - Serving the Community

Without a vision the people [perish], but happy is the
one who follows instruction.
Proverbs 29:18

When I was in Houston, my life seemed directionless and depression set in strong. I needed answers about where I was supposed to be. It was a tough time for me. I turned to one woman I knew would have a word of encouragement and wisdom: my grandmother.

She said, "Son, just come on back home."

The sound of her voice, the strength of her spirit, and the call to return made Mississippi feel like outstretched arms, welcoming me back. I went home and was immediately blessed with a job in my career. I hadn't even applied for the job. It just fell in my lap. When I graduated from college, the placement team had all of the graduates put their resumes on CareerBuilder.com. Unbeknownst to me, my resume was still on the site, getting hits from potential employers. This company saw me and decided to call me for an interview.

I was so young at the time. I couldn't have been more than 26. The job changed my life. I was making six figures yearly. Coming from my town, it was more than three times the average salary in my area.

I had more money than I ever had in my life with no idea what to do with it. So, I spent it. I blew so much money in those early months, it was mind-blowing. I just spent and spent on material things that didn't really matter and held very little value.

The second year that I was working on the job, I went to file my taxes. The tax preparer looked at me and then looked at my paperwork.

"Hold on for a minute," she said as she got up to leave the room.

A few minutes later, several police cars pulled up along with other investigators. She had sounded the alarm that I was a fraud or a thief, getting the law to come and check me out. She couldn't believe that someone like me could earn such an income. She actually let her true feelings slip out of her mouth:

"I just don't see a Black man your age making this type of money living in Yazoo City. That is unheard of."

I remained calm and spoke to the officers to explain. "My job is not in Yazoo City. I travel around the world building nuclear plants, coal plants, and natural gas plants. I obtained this position through the degree I received." I explained it all to them.

They didn't care.

I was just a young Black boy to them. At the time, I had braids in my hair. To them, I gave off a thug look. They unceremoniously handcuffed me and threw me into the back of a police car. For hours and hours, I was detained as they searched for something they could charge me with.

But, through it all, I had the demeanor of an educated, polite, and respectful man. After several phone calls and a lengthy investigation, including a call to the F. B. I., they determined that I was legitimate. I was released without so much as a thank you or and I'm sorry. It was a horrifying experience.

Society claims that it wants people of color to do well, avoid crime, earn a living, and give back to the community. But in reality, society has placed artificial limits on how well people of color are allowed to do. They didn't want a man like me to rise above them in any way and couldn't stomach the idea that I outearned them.

That was my first taste of racial profiling after years and years of feeling safe in my community. I never told anyone about this story. I was too ashamed and disgusted by it.

A year later, I still had the job. I was a regular laborer when I arrived. But I had a mindset that I would not settle for the job I had. I always believed in eyeing the next position and working toward it. So, I ended up working my way up from a laborer to a junior foreman. There were men who had been with the company for a decade who were on my team.

I got to thinking, I'm making all this money and have virtually no expenses. Yet, when I go home, I only have this week's paycheck in my pocket. How can I be earning six figures and still living paycheck to paycheck? How is that even possible?

I wasn't unhappy with the job I had. I wasn't unhappy at all, really. It is just that, when you are not living in purpose, you don't feel fulfilled. Even good things feel hollow. Purposelessness brings a sense of futility to life. You live in the dull grays rather than vivid technicolor. Beyond that, though the job was great, it kept me far, far away from home for long, long periods of time. For nine to ten months out of the year, I was essentially not a part of her life. I could buy her anything she asked for. But what she asked for was my presence. That was something no amount of money could buy. I missed school plays, music recitals, birthdays, and all the other special days she was experiencing without me. If it was my purpose to be a father, how could I justify being happy about the job that robbed me of that joy and responsibility?

It was bad enough that I had only been with my daughter for the first year of her life and was now away from her for long stretches of time.

I remember as if it was yesterday the time I went to a basketball game. I was shocked to see my daughter in the arms of her mother at the same game. I was overjoyed and rushed over to greet her. But when I picked my daughter up, she screamed at the top of her lungs and wriggled her body to get away from me. From that point on, I tried to buy her love by having a good job and money enough to give her anything she wanted.

It was no longer acceptable to live that way. I went to my grandmother's apartment. I laid down in her guest room, staring up at the ceiling. I suddenly noticed something. Before my mother went to prison, she purchased a book that was a Bible guide, and there it was sitting on the dresser across from me. My mother had outlined certain passages in the book. She had placed each one of her kids' names beside certain Bible passages. I read each one she selected for her children. But I was curious to see which one she had chosen for me. Imagine my surprise to learn that he had chosen several. But the one that stood out was:

6 Now godliness with contentment is great gain. 7 For we brought nothing into this world, and it is certain we can carry nothing out. 8 And having food and clothing, with these we shall be content. 9 But those who desire to be rich fall into temptation and a snare, and into many foolish and harmful lusts which drown men in destruction and perdition. 10 For the love of money is a root of all kinds of evil, for which some have strayed from the faith in their greediness and pierced themselves through with many sorrows. 11 But you, O man of God, flee these things and pursue righteousness, godliness, faith, love, patience, gentleness. 12 Fight the good fight of faith, lay hold on eternal life, to which you were also called and have confessed the good confession in the presence of many witnesses. 13 I urge you in the sight of God who gives life to all things, and before Christ Jesus who witnessed the good confession before Pontius Pilate, 14 that you keep this commandment without spot, blameless until our Lord Jesus Christ's appearing.

1 Timothy 6:6-14 (New King James Version)

I was always ambitious and willing to work hard. Mom wanted me to stay uncorrupted by the trappings and lure of money. So, she marked that scripture and made it her prayer for me.

Suddenly, the wisdom of it all came flooding to me. Money is a powerful drug. In many ways, it surpasses other forms of intoxication because it is there wherever you turn. Money can manipulate an otherwise pure mind and can have you do things you wouldn't ordinarily do. People have betrayed those they love for money. People have compromised their principles for money. And people have killed and destroyed in the name of money. Greed is an evil aphrodisiac. It can lead one to do the most sinful things.

I realized that I had a purpose, but my money had no purpose. Since my money had no mission in the world, it was doing every kind of wicked thing from illegal drugs to betting on dog fights and buying for friends the very things that would destroy them.

I was shocked. It was as if my mother knew that I would face these temptations. I continued reading through the Bible booklet as tears flowed over my cheeks and down my chest. I decided that day to be a man of God, a man of love, a man of peace, and a man of integrity. I vowed to pursue a life of spirituality and service. I was renewed and reborn. That does not mean I am a saint. But it does mean that I am committed to a path.

It was high time for me to make such a major shift. I had come from a great family who taught me everything I needed to be successful and survive in the world. I wanted to honor them with my life. Beyond that, I had a daughter who was looking to me for guidance.

So many people live all their lives without ever finding their purpose. I had to get busy walking in my purpose. I had wanted to be a basketball player when I was young, but that dream was dead. I wanted to go into the Air Force, but God said no. It was time for me to embrace my purpose.

A year later, a family in Tennessee lost their home to a fire. It was a couple with twelve children. They lost everything. And the fire occurred just before school started. Those children had none of the things they needed for school. They didn't even have a home to live in. When I saw the news reports, I was stirred. So many times we watch the news claiming that we have to stay informed about what is going on in the world. But then we usually don't do anything about the information we learned. But that day, I was spurred to action.

I thought, *You know what? I have at least $30,000 sitting in my bank account. I am not in want of anything. I have a nice car, plenty of clothes, and all the possessions I could ask for. Why don't I truly become a giver?*

I jumped in my car and drove from Mississippi to Tennessee and tried to find this family. When I did, I blessed them. I brought them school supplies and clothes. And I handed the mother a check for $5000. They broke out in tears of love and happiness. They were overwhelmed with the love and joy I brought. The gifts were less important to them than the sense that someone thought of them and cared about their plight. I sobbed with them.

That is when the lightbulb came on; I had found my purpose. God wanted me to be a leader and a pillar in my community. He wanted blessing to flow *through* me, not just *to* me. I was a conduit of many gifts to those near and far. I was alive with purpose and feeling the fire that comes with intention. The world was new to me in that moment. My life — every moment of it — all came clear and synergized in one moment: past, present, and future. I understood why I suffered like I did. I understood why I had been blessed the way I was. And I understood what was different about me.

From that day to this one, my life has centered around who I can help. I search for those pain points in society and try to apply a healing balm of charity and grace. God wanted me to be the one who searched for the elderly, less fortunate, disadvantaged, and impoverished members of the community.

When I got back to Mississippi, I started making plans for Thanksgiving understanding that it was time when many families suffered a double blow. Not only did they lack the lavish table spread with good food to eat, but they also had to suffer through the shame of knowing that their neighbors were celebrating and giving thanks. I wanted to put that back in balance.

My cousin and I went to the community center in Yazoo City. Together, we rented out the entire space. We secured 500 turkeys that we were able to give away to seniors. But that wasn't enough. I wanted to be sure anyone who was hungry on Thanksgiving or who just wanted something more than a regular meal could have that lavish spread. We prepared and served the Thanksgiving meal for the entire town. Everyone was welcome to sit at the table. Everyone ate for free! I have continued that tradition year after year.

But that wasn't all. I wanted everyone to feel enriched. The boys got free haircuts and I gave away flat screen TVs and game systems that were gifted to the kids via a raffle system. It was like Christmas and Thanksgiving wrapped up in one.

When I completed the first event and saw the people standing in line, I broke into tears. More than a thousand people showed up. I had no idea the problem was so severe. I saw so much love, joy, and happiness. I never wanted that feeling to end. I continue to do it now five years later.

What is even more amazing is the way others in the community have joined the cause. Many people give money to help defray the cost of the event. Many others donate food and prizes. And plenty of people donate their time, prayers, and support in other ways. I am thankful for them all. I am especially grateful for the folks who cook!   Without these people, our Thanksgiving Community Bash would not be the same. The whole community looks forward to it and it is attended by people from all walks of life: rich or poor.

Brothers for the Community is another great passion of mine. Through this organization, we serve the three high schools in the town by giving away $1000 to a student from each school. The students submit an essay on one of the topics I provide including "What changes might be done to make the community better?" and "What kind of leadership could you offer the community?" The goal is to encourage kids to start thinking about how they might give back. While it's great to get an education and go out and conquer the world. But there is a great utility in kids bringing their knowledge and skills back to their beloved Yazoo City.

At first, I wasn't sure how we were going to provide a meal for people. We thought maybe 100 or more folks would show up and we would have to be ready with a ton of food if we were going to feed them all. And speaking of those 100 people we expected, we had to figure out a way to get the word out around town about what we were doing.

I knew that there were plenty of families with amazing cooks. My family had quite a few. So we put an ad in a newspaper, on Facebook, and anywhere else we could think of that might inform people both that we needed help and that the event would be happening.

The event each year seems to get bigger and bigger. At the first one, we just gave away household products like TVs and crockpots. Little did we know we would be flooded with guests. More than 500 people showed up! I couldn't hold back the tears that rested behind my eyes. It blew me away. I walked around and talked to different people so I could hear their stories. It wasn't just a room filled with people who were there to be greedy or take advantage of our kindness. These people were truly in need. It was an awesome turnout in every possible way success could be measured.

We made the headlines and the local news stations that something great was happening in Yazoo City. Then COVID struck and threatened to put a wrench in our yearly tradition. But I decided that hunger waits for nothing — not even COVID. We just changed the format and had people drive up and receive food in their cars. We still did the raffles and the giveaways as hundreds upon hundreds of cars pulled in to receive food and participate in the fun.

We diligently went through all the essays and picked the ones we thought best expressed the spirit of what we were trying to accomplish. We were not necessarily looking for kids who used perfect grammar. We overlooked technical mistakes because the whole point of this exercise was to find the diamond-in-the-rough. We tried to pick the one that was clearly written by the child (rather than some overeager parent) and the one who captured the heart and spirit of Yazoo City best.

In addition, I knew that each year when school started in August there would be kids without proper uniforms because their parents couldn't afford to buy it for them. We would pick three different families and buy their school uniforms.

School supplies was a no-brainer project. We understood that kids can't succeed if they didn't have the tools they needed. So we got busy pulling those together.

But we wanted to do something for families as a whole that would make a big difference. And it hit us that utility bills were higher in the winter near Christmastime when families could use a bit of disposable income. So, we also filled refrigerators up with groceries for a month and paid utility bills for needy families.

For my community in Yazoo City, this is especially true. We have been forgotten, it seems, by the world. We are 85% African American with some serious concerns. Our schools have had to deal with getting taken over by the state due to poor testing scores. The city suffered massive debt. And we have a lot of young black boys and girls who need and deserve an opportunity.

Many of the kids who get in trouble with school or with the law are simply a product of their environment. They are raised by what they hear on the radio and on TV. Many of them have absent fathers or broken homes. They easily get caught up in a lifestyle that breaks the spirit. But their minds are strong. They are capable. They just need a hand. Some of our boys are caught up in the thug lifestyle that will lead to prison or the grave. Many of our girls are babies raising babies because they went looking for a man's love in the wrong place.

I can't blame them. I will leave the blame game for others. For me, I want to do all I can to help them… save them… or at least provide an open door to something bigger and better. That is what I strive to do daily. That is what my cousin Richard and the other group of coaches he works with have been doing. They are literally taking kids off the streets and giving them proper coaching and training from guys who care about them and want to see them succeed. They are essentially teaching boys to be men. Of course, they want to win games. But the program does not center around winning football games.

It's about being together, learning, and teaching. By example, they are showing kids that they don't have to sell drugs and do all the illegal things to make an earnest living. They have options if they want to have the money, the fine clothes, the nice shoes, and other material things. They don't have to jeopardize their freedom to get it.

It's amazing to see the kids come home from school and rush right back out to get to practice. They only stay home long enough to bathe and change. The parents can feel confident that the kids are someplace safe learning skills that will help to take them through life.

But community service is not all rainbows and sunshine. There is a definite dark side. Sadly, I was introduced to that dark side when I got to see the corruption that infested the political world in my town. I couldn't understand how I could help the needy and the poor when the city had access to more resources than I did. Our city council had too many people with the wrong motive for serving.

I looked to heaven and thanked God that he gave me brains, a heart, and a conscience. I set my intention to prove that leaders could be people of moral, ethics, and values. With that, I started my campaign, becoming the youngest Alderman and Mayor Pro Tem in the history of the state of Mississippi. I am working hard to undo the damage that has been done to my community over the years. Everyone knows who I am and what I stand for. They trust that I am able and willing to bring changes to the community.

The politics in a small town can be tricky. There is so much that comes into play beyond doing what is best for the town. It's kind of different from the politics we see on CNN and other places in the national media. The government often passes laws that should trickle down to communities like Yazoo City. When it gets to a local government situation, we should be able to adapt to those changes. This often refers to funding. Sadly, it doesn't always make it to the small communities. The government spends billions and trillions. But towns like ours never see a dime.

When governors receive funds, they're allowed to take in money that's broken down into municipalities for the citizens of each State. But that is not what always happens. The governor can have $300 billion sent to him or her, but how it gets filtered around the state depends on a bunch of other issues... usually politics.

Once they break the money down, they pick and choose who gets what. From the outside looking in, it's corrupt. From the inside, it's even worse. From the nation down to the local arena, we need people of honor handling government business.

I try my best to put as much as possible into the poverty-stricken areas of town. We must lift each other up if we expect to attract new families and Fortune 500 businesses. Today, if they look at my hometown, they will see the poverty rate and choose elsewhere. They won't invest in a town that is run down and where there is no housing for their employees or development happening at the level of city hall.

We are a community of 10,000-strong. But that is small to a company with thousands of employees. We need to show them all the reasons why Yazoo City is the best place to do business. That is how we continue to support small, local businesses while courting large corporations to help build the city. That is my vision. As a result, the people living here will have a better quality of life.

Chapter 15 - Quiet Mentoring

"A mentor is someone who allows you to see the hope inside yourself." — Oprah Winfrey.

The mentoring I do and believe so strongly is the quiet kind. It is the day to day life that is lived where others can see and know that you care about them. It is your commitment to give folks an opportunity to be proud of themselves and proud of their city.

With sports being such a major component in my life, I wanted to do all I could to help bring more sports to the area, so we also support the football team which today has around 200 young boys from the Community participating every year. Since basketball was my thing — not football — I turned everything over to my cousins Richard and Jonathan who have full control of the program and do an amazing job with it. It is clear that their work is having a major impact in the Community right now.

I love both of them for all they do and commend them for it every time I see them. What they have done in the lives of these kids is immeasurable.

It is the way you love in a crisis when people need you the most and don't even know all the ways in which you can help.

In 2020, Yazoo City was hit with the COVID pandemic. People were understandably scared, and it was a difficult time for everyone. Lots of people didn't want to be touched, and they struggled to cope with the situation. People were dying all around us, and the images on television of bodies stacked high waiting to be buried or cremated terrified everyone.

Yazoo City was accustomed to being a close-knit community. But COVID forced us all indoors and took away many of the events we have come to know and love. But the pandemic could not stop the heart of charity from beating strong. If anything, COVID strengthened us. During the height of the pandemic, we did checks on our community's seniors to make sure people had food, water, and other supplies.

If I was out at a grocery store, I would post a note out on Facebook for anyone who was needing anything from the grocery store. That way, they didn't have to venture out and risk catching the virus. During that time, we brought food and medical supplies to many and simply dropped it off on their porches.

The first Thanksgiving we were able to come back together for a meal after COVID was fun but strange. First, we didn't know what the outcome was going to be. People didn't know for sure how safe it was to be around each other. Besides, the guidelines at the Community Center mandated that we stay six feet apart from each other. And, we were only allowed to have a certain number of people in the building at one time. We were surprised to see that people still came out. It felt as if it took forever to serve everyone, but we got it done.

Having an impact on someone else's life is a feeling beyond words. When we can know for sure that we have changed someone's life or made their day, we become a different person because we take the experience of meeting them along with the love and gratitude they show us everywhere we go. Yes, people need "things" like money, food, water, etc. But what they really need are other people showing that they care.

I go to a few of these football practices and talk to some of these guys when they have a break. These young boys are the same ones I see on the streets. They know me. They trust me.

From time to time, one will get reckless and will need to be pulled to the side for a loving talk. After a short talk with them about morals, values, respect, and their futures, they usually straighten up. They all know that I am not afraid to tell them to pull up their pants and not have them hanging off their behinds showing their underwear. This is the kind of behavior kids do to test the love of the community. If no one speaks up, it confirms what they already think: that no one cares.

When the kids see me on the street, they know I am there for them and that I care. After all, they can't miss me. I get out and ride the neighborhoods in my F150. If they are up to no good, they won't continue to misbehave if they see that big truck roll by. And they always, always pull up their pants!

The act of mentoring is not easy. It can often feel like a lot of pressure because you want to be the best you can be and worry that you can't live up to the standard. But quiet mentoring is simply living as a loving member of a community and giving your best — whatever that is. It means being willing to let people see your heroism as well as your humanity. Nothing is more powerful than a man who can say he was wrong, apologize, and make a commitment to do better.

Chapter 16 – My Vision

"When I dare to be powerful, to use my strength in the
service of my vision, then it becomes less and less important
whether I am afraid."
— Audre Lorde

I have set three goals for myself. Before I tell you what they are, allow me to share why I set the goals in the first place. Goals are like the rudder of a boat. It doesn't matter if the boat is powered by a high-speed motor, unless it is being steered in a particular direction, there is no telling where it will end up. Speed and goals are not necessarily correlated, I would much rather have a set of good old-fashioned oars that help me move the boat in a determined direction than have a motor with no rudder.

Goals push us to think outside of our normal human limitations. After all, we are capable of so much more than we imagine. Goals take us to that place that we must first visit in our minds. If we can see it, we can be it. Once we have visioned it in our heads and hearts, the rest is fairly easy. All that is left is hard work.

Back to my three goals… These are goals I prayed earnestly for. So many people live their whole lives for one thing only to find out that it was not their true purpose and destiny. After decades of climbing the ladder, they reach the top only to find out that the ladder was leaning against the wrong wall. They end up in their later years battling regret from having done what they shouldn't have — and having not done what they should have.

But, today, I am certain that I have found my place in the world and know what my contributions need to be. The first was running for public office. I knew that I needed to live a life of service to communities around my city, state, and country.

The second was to write this book. I knew that my story was meant to be shared and would have an impact on those who read it. I was meant to be a voice of hope — a testament to hope and an encouragement to those who need to know that how we start is not necessarily how we will find. Each decision along the way is meant to be a course correction on a trajectory to the ultimate destiny.

My third and final goal is to establish an open a homeless shelter here in my town. Homelessness is such a pervasive issue that many people don't understand. They walk or drive by those on the streets and shake their heads in condemnation, never understanding what it took to get there and how hard it is to come back to being homed once you start living in shelters or on the streets. I hope to be able to secure the shelter in the next few years and provide more than a place to live. The homeless require a broad range of services including medical care, mental healthcare, employment training, money management, and social skills. Coming back from homelessness is like being reborn; you must learn to walk again.

The funding for the goals I have set is a work in progress. I have been blessed to be able to fund this book. But my other goals are still hanging in the balance. The massive costs associated with campaigns and homelessness services can be substantial. But, with the help of my organization and supporters, we will get this. This homeless shelter is not going to be your typical homeless shelter. Many of them are unisex and cause families to be separated. We want to do the opposite and allow families to bring their children to stay for a period of time.

Another facet of homelessness is sometimes the presence of substance abuse and domestic violence, which was the direct cause of their homelessness. Whatever the situation is, this shelter is meant to be a safe haven for those who want to get established. Those who have drug and alcohol problems can come and get the help they so desperately need.

I have already started the process on all three goals. You are holding my book in your hands, I am mounting my mayoral campaign, and I am in search of a site where I could build the shelter.

I am certain that, once all three goals are reached, God will give me a vision for what is next. We never know all that He has in store for us. We follow Him and trust that He knows where our gifts can be best used.

In the coming pages, you will see the harrowing journey that has given rise to these goals and that have made me who I am. I trust that you will see a bit of yourself in my story and understand that nothing is impossible for you.

Chapter 17 - The love Dream

"Twenty years from now you will be more disappointed
by the things that you didn't do than by the ones you did do. So
throw off the bowlines. Sail away from the safe harbor. Catch the
trade winds in your sails. Explore. Dream. Discover."
— *H. Jackson Brown Jr., P.S. I Love You*

For the past few years, I struggled with sleep more than I had even in prior years. To help, I took medication but found myself getting addicted to sleeping aids. I had been tormented by the past I had experienced. Going to sleep and staying asleep as long as I could had become an escape from the burdens, fears, and awful memories that haunted me in the night.

When I woke up in the morning, I was in hot pursuit of living my dreams in real life. But when I tried to shut it all down at the end of the day, it became harder and harder to quiet my mind and settle my troubled spirit. When sleep finally came, it brought with it horrifying dreams that plagued me and made my sleep restless. I spent a lot of time in prayer about this and God answered with a new dream that I named the "Love Dream."

99

In these dreams, I wasn't in human form, but in a spiritual form. As far as I could tell, the spirit form was that of masculine love. But there was also another spirit present, a feminine one. This spirit was nothing like anything I had ever experienced before. It was calm, peaceful, loving, and provided what felt like a safe haven for me.

While in my dreams, I was in my rawest, truest form whenever I was in the presence of this feminine spirit. It was the only thing that made me feel like I could be myself and, more importantly, I felt the closest to God whenever I was in the presence of this other spirit.

I spent a lot of time thinking about this recurring dream and what it might mean. Whenever I was awake, I prayed, asking God to make it make sense. My best explanation was that this had to be what God's true love was for me and what it might feel like to be in God's presence. Weeks, sometimes months, passed without having this same dream even once. But then the dream would return. When it did, we picked up exactly where we left off.

My prayer is that God would allow me to be the person who is worthy of the feeling in this dream in real life. I want to emanate that pure and radiant love to everyone. I want people to feel at ease in my presence and know that they are safe. And I want to honor God through everything I do.

Day-by-day as an elected official, I find myself changing and becoming the man God made me to be. Even though I've gained tons of support, there have been forces at work overtime to discourage me from my leadership duties. But I want to allow this to happen in God's timing and in His way. My ultimate goal is to one day be the Mayor of my city. I feel that may be the final and greatest accomplishment of my purpose in life. But I don't know for sure all that He has in store for me. I have learned to walk with Him rather than run ahead of Him or lag behind.

I've become a loner. I find that I spend 90% of my time alone. Part of my reason for being alone is because I don't want to ever let people down. I value other peoples' opinions of me. However, being alone is not the same as being lonely. When I walk with God, I know that he is always there beside me. If I continue to give my all, I will prosper... I will succeed.

Conclusion

The greatest glory in living lies not in never falling, but in rising every time we fall. -Nelson Mandela

I've got footsteps. So do you. We have all carved a path, whether faint or thick, from the path we have walked. Just as a baby can walk in the sand beside her father, each will leave evidence that they were there. The question for you and me is whether or not we will leave footsteps that are big enough, distinct enough, and durable enough for others to walk in. My prayer is that I have made huge footsteps anyone can see and follow to the next place in their journey. If the generations that follow me can see something in my life that inspires them, my living will not have been in vain, and all of my trials will have been more than worth it.

That is what legacy is all about. It is the ability to reach outside of your life and pass something of value to someone else. If you're lucky (and smart) you will pass on value to many others and shape their lives just as many who have gone before have shaped yours.

Yazoo City has been a major part of that journey. No matter what Disney says, Yazoo City is the best place on earth with the best people and the best opportunities to make friends and build family. Serving this place has been the source of deep pride for me for many years and is the source of great hope for my future in this amazing place.

My life has been shaped by so many different influences. Each has impacted me in a different way and led me to the place I am today. Each situation was a learning experience. Whether it felt pleasant at the time or not, it was good. Good that I went through it. Good that I survived it. And good that I learned something from it.

We are not promised all sunshine and lollipops. It's one of the greatest fallacies of positive thinking. We assume that we can somehow wish away trouble and difficulty. We cannot. Life is good, but it is always dotted by suffering. But without suffering, we would never know what true joy is. Suffering provides that much-needed contrast and reminds us to stop, look up, and say thank you for the sunshine.

ABOUT THE AUTHOR

Macklyn Austin is the quintessential success story. From a traumatic past, he has been able to build an extraordinary life, rising to serve as Vice-Mayor of Yazoo City, Mississippi.

Macklyn "Mack" Austin is a businessman who serves in his official seat as Yazoo City's Ward 2 Alderman.

He balances his challenging work in politics with a career in industry, family, and a devotion to community service. He is a passionate writer with a warrior's spirit who enjoys uplifting and empowering others, giving to those in need, and being a blessing to all who cross his path.

Macklyn cherishes his two beautiful daughters, his mother, Shirley, and his grandmother Alice who have all served as the inspiration for his life and work. Most of all, he honors God for His divine protection, grace, and mercy. Macklyn currently resides in Yazoo City, Mississippi where he believes he is destined to remain a beacon of hope to his community.

You can reach Macklyn Austin at:

Macklyn@sbcglobal.net
Facebook: Macklyn Austin
Instagram: macklyn_austin

ABOUT YAZOO CITY

Yazoo City is a small town that packs a big punch. At just under ten square miles, there is so much to see and do in this historic town which got its name in 1682 in honor of the Yazoo tribe living there. But it was founded much later in 1824 when its name was changed from Manchester to Yazoo City. Its population is just over 10,000 people as of the 2020 census. But it is a great place for people around Mississippi and beyond to visit.

Yazoo City has been a big part of American history, serving as an important location for the Confederate Shipyard and was the location of heavy fighting in the Civil war in the 1860s, a devastating fire in 1904, and a flood in 1927 — each destroying much of the city.

The city came together to rebuild both times.

Today, Yazoo City has much to offer the eye and the palate. Main Street in the center of town is one of the biggest attractions of the city. Historic buildings were painted in various colors lending an artistic flair to the city's center. The Main Street hotel is a major attraction that draws both guests and admirers of its architecture.

Yazoo City is the Delta's gateway. It maintains the old-world spirit with a generous helping of modern touches.

If you enjoyed this book, please help others find it by leaving a review on the site where you purchased it.

Thank you for your support!

Made in the USA
Columbia, SC
08 February 2025

53550452R00072